T0402825

About This Book

Title: *Weather Patterns*

Step: 6

Word Count: 242

Skills in Focus: R-controlled e

Tricky Words: Earth, season, water, into, leaves, again, come, fall, sky

Ideas For Using This Book

Before Reading:

- **Comprehension:** Look at the title and cover image together. Walk through the pictures in the book with readers and have them make predictions about what they might learn in the book.
- **Accuracy:** Practice saying the tricky words listed on page 1.
- **Phonics:** Tell students they will read words with the r-controlled vowel *e* spelled *er*. Have students look at the word *weather* in the title on the front cover. Help readers point to both of the letters in the word that say /r/. Explain to readers that the spelling *er* includes an *e*, but we only hear /r/, not the sounds we might expect *e* to make. Write this word on the piece of paper, underlining the letters that represent the target sound. Repeat with story words such as *cover, summer, winter,* and *perch.* Have readers look through the first few pages of the book to see if they can find any other examples of words that have the *er* spelling pattern.

During Reading:

- Have readers point under each word as they read it.
- **Decoding:** If readers are stuck on a word, help them say each sound and blend the sounds together smoothly. Be sure to point out words with the r-controlled *e* as they appear.
- **Comprehension:** Invite readers to talk about new things they are learning about weather patterns while reading. What are they learning that they didn't know before?

After Reading:

Discuss the book. Some ideas for questions:

- What are the different kinds of weather? What is the weather like in different seasons?
- What do you still wonder about weather?

Weather Patterns

Text by Laura Stickney

Reading Consultant
Deborah MacPhee, PhD
Professor, School of Teaching and Learning
Illinois State University

PICTURE WINDOW BOOKS
a capstone imprint

What Is Weather?
Weather is the state of the air outside. It can be hot or cold.

It can be wet or dry.
Some days are hotter
and some are colder.

Earth has
weather patterns.

Weather shifts each day.

On some days,
the weather is dry.

The sun is out.
Rivers glitter
in the sun.

On some days,
the weather is wet.

It rains. Rivers get choppy.

The Seasons

Weather patterns change each season.

Earth has
four seasons.

First is winter. In winter, the sky gets darker.

Water freezes into ice.
Snow and sleet fall
from the sky.

Nights are longer in winter. Days are shorter.

In winter, the wind makes us shiver. We need coats and hats to cover up.

After winter is spring.
In spring, snow melts.

Flowers grow.
Plants turn green.

Critters come out. Snakes slither. Birds chitter and chatter.

Birds perch in trees and
preen their feathers.
They lay eggs.

In summer, the weather gets hotter. The sun shines bright.

It makes things hot.

You need to stay
cool in summer.
Put on a hat.

Cover your skin
with sunscreen.
That way, the
sun will not
burn your skin.

Nights are shorter in summer.
Days are longer.

There are storms and rain in summer.

In fall, the weather
gets cooler.
The wind whispers
and feels chilly.

Leaves on
trees get crisp
and brown.
They fall to
the ground.

After fall, it is winter again.
The seasons start over.

More Ideas:

Phonics Activity

Writing with r-controlled *e*:
Ask readers to write a story using as many words as possible that have the *er* letter combination. The story can be as silly or serious as readers want!

Suggested words: weather, feather, whisper, shiver, cover, critter, darker, shorter

Extended Learning Activity

Compare and Contrast:
Ask readers to draw a chart with four sections labeled with the names of the seasons. Then ask readers to write what they know about each season inside the sections. Readers could also draw pictures of what the weather is like in that season. Challenge readers to use words with *er* letter combinations in their descriptions.

Published by Picture Window Books, an imprint of Capstone
1710 Roe Crest Drive, North Mankato, Minnesota 56003
capstonepub.com

Library of Congress Cataloging-in-Publication Data is available
on the Library of Congress website.

ISBN: 9798875227226 (hardback)
ISBN: 9798875231131 (paperback)
ISBN: 9798875231117 (eBook PDF)

Image Credits: iStock: AlinaMD, 22–23, DjelicS, 28–29, FatCamera, 14,
Meindert van der Haven, 26–27, Shironosov, 17, 32, Standret, 30–31,
Tbradford, 4; Shutterstock: Akin Ozcan, 10–11, Andrei Stepanov, 15, Deborah
Lee Rossiter, 19, FotoHelin, 12–13, Gerald A. DeBoer, 20, m_bumbik, 16,
MarKord, 24–25, Natalia Kokhanova, 18, Pressmaster, cover, Riedal, 8–9,
Santipong Srikhamta, 5, Sergey Novikov, 2–3, Sondem, 6–7, Yvontrep, 1, 21

Printed and bound in China.   6274